ON

THE EDUCATION OF WOMEN.

A Paper

READ BY

MRS. WILLIAM GREY,

AT THE

MEETING OF THE SOCIETY OF ARTS,

MAY 31st, 1871.

WITH AN APPENDIX.

LONDON:

WILLIAM RIDGWAY, 169, PICCADILLY. W.

1871.

Price One Shilling.

THE EDUCATION OF WOMEN.*

THE subject I have specially to call your attention to this evening is the low condition of female education, the inadequate provision made for it out of the endowments of the country, and the difficulty of obtaining support from the general public for any scheme having for its object the higher education of women.

In what I have to say, I shall only touch very slightly on the classes which come under the Elementary Education Act, and for this reason, that in those classes girls do, on the whole, share all the educational advantages equally with the boys.

* This paper is republished from the Journal of the Society of Arts, with only such slight alterations and omissions as were suggested by a more careful revision. I have added in the Appendix some of the detailed evidence I was obliged to omit in reading for want of time.

They receive the same instruction, with the addition of sewing; they are examined by the same inspectors and by the same standards; their teachers undergo the same special training for their work, and receive the same certificate of efficiency. In their case, therefore, there is no special grievance to complain of. The inferiority of girls' schools of that class, and of the results obtained in in them, is due, where it exists, to the general causes which affect women's education as a whole, causes which I propose to point out further on, and which can be removed only by a change in the public opinion whence they spring. It is, then, to the education given to girls in all schools above the elementary schools, that I propose to dwell this evening. I shall leave theories aside, and bring before you facts resting upon authority which cannot be questioned; and the main source I have drawn upon is the volume before you, containing Reports of the Schools Inquiry Commission on the Education of Girls, together with the evidence given before the Commissioners by ladies of tried ability and great experience in the education of their own sex.* †To these I have added extracts from

---

* Reports issued by the Schools Inquiry Commission on the Education of Girls, reprinted with the sanction of H. M.'s Commissioners, with extracts of the evidence and a preface by D. Beale, Principal of the Ladies' College, Cheltenham. London: Nutt, 270, Strand.

† Appendix I.

the evidence given before the Commissioners by various gentlemen interested in education. The reports were collected and reprinted in the convenient shape you see here, with the sanction of her Majesty's Commissioners, by Miss Beale, who is at the head of a most successful educational institute for girls—the Ladies' College at Cheltenham—one of the very few proprietary schools for girls in the country; and Miss Beale has added to the volume a very valuable preface, giving the results of her own large experience, and adding all the weight of her testimony to the truth of the sad picture presented by the reports.

The Commissioners, in their General Report, sum up the result of the Assistant-Commissioners' inquiries in the following words:— " Want of thoroughness and foundation ; want of system ; slovenliness and showy superficiality ; inattention to rudiments ; undue time given to accomplishments, and those not taught intelligently, or in any scientific manner; want of organisation."

Mr. Norris's evidence, quoted in the above Report as the most concise and accurate view of the state of girls' schools, is to this effect:—" We find, as a rule, a very small amount of professional skill, an inferior set of school books, a vast deal of dry, uninteresting task work, rules put into the memory with no explanation of their principles, no system of examination worthy of the name, a very false estimate of the relative value of the several kinds of acquirement, a reference to effect rather than solid worth, a tendency to fill or adorn rather than to strengthen the mind." Taking these points more in detail, I will try to reproduce, in slight but accurate outline, the picture given in this volume of the education by which the future wives and mothers of the lower and upper middle-classes of this country, and the large and ever-increasing number of single women who have to earn their own bread, and often the bread of others, are trained for their work in life. I must first, however, remind you that the standard of comparison by which the inspectors judged the education of girls was not any standard of ideal or theoretical perfection, but that of the education given to boys in the same grades of society,—an education which, according to Mr. Matthew Arnold, leaves our young men of the upper classes barbarians; of the middle class, Philistines; of the lower class, heathens. Without accepting this extreme view, it is abundantly evident from the reports of the Schools Inquiry Commission, that the standard is not a high one, and that nothing can give so deplorable a measure of the low condition of girls' education as the fact that it is unanimously pronounced, on the best authority, to be very inferior to that of boys.

The only points on which this judgment is reversed in favour of the girls are reading and spelling. The reading is almost invariably spoken of as good. As regards religious knowledge, again, the evidence is not unfavourable, and it is worth noticing that the religious difficulty is even less felt in girls' schools than in boys' schools. The religious knowledge, however, for which the girls get credit seems to be little more than a tolerably accurate acquaintance with the facts of Scripture history and the outlines of the Christian faith, and cannot therefore rank high as an element of education. As regards the mere facts of history and geography the girls are sometimes better than the boys; but, with rare exceptions, the teaching is superficial, and from miserable catechisms or compendiums of knowledge, such as "Mangnall's Questions," and others of the same type.*

With regard to grammar, Mr. Bryce's statement expresses the substance of all the reports on the subject. He says:—"In four-fifths of the schools, both higher and lower, English grammar means the committal to memory of Lindley Murray, or of some one of his less illustrious brethren, and it was surprising to see how little notion even intelligent teachers had of handling the subject in a rational way."†

The arithmetic is even more unsatisfactory than the grammar. The Commissioners, in their general report, refer to it as the "weak point" in women teachers. Mr. Bryce says "the teaching in

* Appendix II.　　　† Appendix III.

this subject is poor, slow, unintelligent; to speak more correctly, there is no teaching, only a languid working of sums." "I feel quite certain," says Mr. Fearon, "that if the girls in half a dozen of the best national schools, formerly under my inspection, were tried in elementary arithmetic against the young ladies of an equal age in half a dozen of the best schools that I examined, the national schools would produce better results." It would be tedious to multiply quotations all repeating the same testimony. I would only remark, that this arithmetical deficiency in girls' schools does not appear to be owing to any natural inaptitude, for where the teaching was good, the girls proved themselves equal and even superior to the boys.*

Physical science has a place in girls' schools, but Mr. Bompas found it only "a subject for lectures." Mr. Giffard reports it "as read only from text-books;" and Mr. Fitch says that "it is nowhere taught systematically, and that it is commonly unintelligible." After mentioning that astronomy and the use of the globes, by some curious law, seem to be recognised as constituting the one department of science specially interesting to girls, he adds, "few things are sadder than to find how the sublimest of all physical sciences is vulgarised in ladies' schools."†

Modern languages and music, to which, according to Mr. Fitch, one-third of a girl's school life is devoted, fare little better.

* Appendix IV.　　　　　† Appendix V.

"In fashionable schools," says Mr. Bryce, "girls of good abilities, when they leave school at 17, can usually translate an ordinary author with some facility, and turn an easy phrase of English into French, which, if neither idiomatic nor accurate, is at least intelligible." . . . . "It is quite exceptional to find them able to do more than this, that is to say, to write a theme in French, or to show such a familiarity with words and phrases as would enable them to keep up a conversation for ten minutes."

Mr. Fearon says:—" Young ladies of 16 or 18, whose parents were paying from £100 to £150 a year for their education, were found ignorant of the inflections of the most common irregular verbs, and unable to turn a simple sentence into French without blunders."

The specimens given are almost incredible, and, for that reason, I should have been glad to quote them verbatim, but must refrain from want of time.* Two of the assistant-commissioners class French with arithmetic as the weak points in the school teaching of girls, a result not a little astonishing, considering that it is one of the two subjects (music being the other) which are considered by parents all-important in a girl's education.

But though such stress is laid upon music, though commissioner after commissioner complains of the manner in which it interferes with other

* Appendix VI.

studies by the time it requires, and with the discipline of a school by the impossibility of teaching it in class, music is apparently no better taught, as a rule, than French.

Mr. Bryce says he was assured that the common way of teaching it was not "only unscientific but irrational and wasteful." The same opinion is given by other inspectors, yet Mr. Bryce adds:—— " At present music occupies pretty nearly as much of a girl's life as classics do of a boy's."*

Drawing, of course, is taught with an equal disregard to thoroughness, to scientific principles, and to the cultivation of artistic feeling and taste, and it has, besides, this disadvantage, that the common practice of masters in touching up their pupils' performances for exhibition at home fosters a habit of dishonesty, and that too prevalent tendency running through the whole of female education, the tendency to care more for appearance than reality, to seem rather than to be. I will now give you some of the general results of their inspection of girls' schools expressed by the different assistant-commissioners.

" It is no exaggeration to say," states Mr. Fitch, " that in the mass of girls' schools the intellectual aims are very low, and the attainments lower than the aims. The course of instruction is very narrow. It leaves many of the pupils' best faculties unused. . . . If the reproach be just that women do not

* Appendix VII.

reason accurately, and that their knowledge, even when they possess it, is deficient in organic unity, in coherence, and in depth, there is no need to look for any recondite explanation of the fact. The state of the schools in which they are educated sufficiently explains it."*

Mr. Stanton says:—" The ignorance in many of these lower and middle class schools was most profound, and I cannot but remember that I probably only saw the better specimens."

Mr. Gifford sums up the impressions he derived from his visits to girls' schools thus:—" That the mental training of the best girls' schools is unmistakably inferior to that of the best boys' schools; and the great and obvious feature of all girls' schools, except those of the very humblest, is the enormous preponderance given to accomplishments."

I might multiply these extracts to any extent, but, my time being limited, I will add only a few passages from the reports of Mr. Fearon and Mr. Gifford, whose districts, embracing London and its neighbourhood, and Surrey and Sussex, contained the highest grade girls' schools in the country. Mr. Fearon concludes, as regards schools of the first grade :—(1.) " The provision in London is most inadequate." (2.) " The cost of education is very high." (3.) " The buildings and premises of almost all these schools, whether day or boarding, is most unsatisfactory." " Except Queen's and

* Appendix VIII.

Bedford Colleges, where gentlemen are employed in teaching, and at a very few private schools whose principals have determined to make a stand against the frivolous character of girls' education, the quality of the visiting teachers of language and science is very inferior in girls' schools of the first grade." Further on, after stating that he thought it advisable to pitch his standard in judging of the elementary work in secondary girls' schools not quite so high as he had been used to pitch it in reporting on elementary girls' schools, he says :— " I have no record of any class of girls about twelve years old, in any first grade school that I examined, reaching the standard of *good*."

I will complete this picture of the state of girls' education by some extracts from the evidence given before the Schools Inquiry Commissioners.* Mr. Sargant stated in his evidence—" That the education of girls in Birmingham, of what he terms the middle class, is disgracefully bad; that they are very much worse educated than their brothers —very much worse than those who go to any school under Her Majesty's Inspectors."

Mr. Roche, whose classes in Cadogan Gardens have been attended for years by girls of the higher classes, says—" The defects which I have observed in my pupils, as the result of their previous education, are, a want of grammatical knowledge, even in English, and an indistinct pronunciation of the

* Appendix IX.

mother-tongue. Everything is done by memory, with abominable books of exercises and keys for grammar, of questions and dry answers for history, geography, and astronomy. There is very little development of intellectual faculties."

Miss Emily Davies, now a member of the London School Board, and well known as having devoted herself to the cause of female education, says :— " I have come across the best school-mistresses. They always speak a great deal of the bad preparation of the girls who come to them. They say they are perfectly ignorant. Their ignorance is unfathomable."

Miss Beale, the editor of these reports, states of female education in the class of life to which her pupils belong, *i.e.*, of independent gentlemen and professional men, that " it is defective in an extraordinary degree. That it is worse than that received by persons of a much humbler condition at the national schools;" and, in a note to page 198, she says :—" Some, who produced papers almost inconceivably bad, have, to my knowledge, spent many years at school. . . . . Evidence is afforded that there are expensive schools where pupils who have naturally fair abilities may remain for years without obtaining the rudiments of education. . . . I mean, leave them incapable of writing, spelling, or composing fairly in their own language; almost ignorant of French grammar, and scarcely able to work the simplest sum correctly."

Miss Wolstenholme, herself the mistress of a young ladies' school, says " that from what she hears, she should imagine that, in spite of external accomplishments, the girls of the middle-class really are not very much better educated than girls of the same age in the national schools. They have external accomplishments, but no solid information."

Miss Buss, the principal of the North London Collegiate School for Girls, which she has raised to an endowed school by investing in trust for its benefit the earnings of her 20, years' work there, says, in answer to the question whether she thought that the girls who came to her from the preparatory schools were in a better or worse state of instruction than boys similarly circumstanced, " I do not know about the boys; I know that the girls could not be worse prepared than they are."

Some tables which have been furnished to me by the principal of a large secondary day-school, attended by daughters of tradesmen, clerks, and a few of independent means, give the following results of entrance examinations:—Of 26 girls, whose ages averaged $12\frac{1}{2}$, the number of faults in an easy English dictation of ten lines were about nine to each girl. Out of ten questions in easy arithmetic given to each girl, there was an average of nine incorrect answers. The reading generally was bad. One pupil, not reckoned among the above, who was entered as the daughter of a gentlewoman, could not do anything. She had not been to school, and implied she had not learnt anything.

Mr. Carleton Tufnell, in answer to my request that he would give me the results of his experience, wrote me a letter, of which the following are extracts :*—" Every teacher appointed to a school under the Poor-law Board must undergo an examination, and in this way I have come to know the sort of education which many of the women who apply for these situations have received. The examination is extremely slight. . . . . The questions are not at all more difficult than could be readily answered by any pupil in the first class of an ordinary village school. A first class in a really good village school would go far beyond them. . . . The papers are sometimes so bad that we are only justified in passing the writers by the consideration that if we do not accept them we should get no candidates for the places at all. The candidates are always respectable women of the middle-class, and have sometimes been governesses in private families, yet their writing is often hardly intelligible, and deformed with such mistakes in spelling as would pluck them in any examination for the lowest Civil Service examination. Their Biblical knowledge is excessively meagre, and their arithmetic worst of all, generally not going further than the simple rules, and if they

* Appendix X.

try a sum in multiplication of money, the working commonly shows fatal blunders. Sometimes, seeing that candidates know nothing of these elementary branches of education, I have asked what they do know, and what they have been accustomed to teach in private families. The answer is crochet, the piano, French, Italian. Of course, it is obvious that their knowledge of all these subjects must be extremely limited."

The evidence I have given applies mainly to the middle-class in its three strata, lower, middle, and upper ; but I have reason to believe that, in the higher classes, the gentry and aristocracy, who are mostly educated at home, although the instruction given may be better, and the standard of information somewhat higher, there is just as little systematic training of the intellectual powers, of reason and imagination, just as little appreciation of knowledge, of the higher forms of literature, or of real excellence in the pursuit of any art.

It should be noted that the education given to girls, the result of which I have just laid before you, is exceedingly expensive; the Commissioners in their general report, state that the cost of girls' schooling, where it varies from that of boys of the same class, varies on the side of more expense. Mr. Bryce says " that the charges in first-rate schools in Manchester seem moderate compared with those of the most fashionable London or Brighton schools, but they make a girl's education nearly twice as expensive as that far more solid and practically useful education which a boy receives." So that the practical British parent not only procures for his daughter a very bad article, but pays very highly for it.

It would be gross unfairness to lay the blame of the miserably low standard of education given in girls' schools upon the mistresses. The number of proprietary or endowed schools for girls is very small. The immense majority are private schools, kept by ladies who must live by them, who cannot afford to refuse pupils on the ground of their insufficient preparation, and who must supply the kind of education the pupils' parents are willing to pay for. As Miss Buss says, in her evidence given before the Commissioners, "it is so entirely a matter of necessity for the mistress to live, that she is obliged to allow the children to do as they like, and the parents too." Miss Davies, after saying that many of those she had had to do with were intelligent and conscientious, added :—"They complain very much of their difficulties, and explained their difficulties to be that they have had very imperfect training themselves, and they are hampered by want of money. Very often, too, they are at the mercy of very ignorant parents."

This is the root of the whole matter; there is no demand for a better education for girls. "Although the world has existed several thousand years," says Mr. Bryce, "the notion that women have minds as cultivable and as well worth cultivating as men's minds, is still regarded by the ordinary British parent as an offensive, not to say a revolutionary, paradox." The same Commissioner says, " that he lost no opportunity of inquiring from schoolmistresses their experience in this matter. Their answer was invariably the same. Mothers are acutely sensitive to anything which may affect their daughters' social success, whether it be the 'selectness' of the school or its situation, or the fame of the music or dancing masters. They are profoundly indifferent to their diligence (as a moral quality), or to their progress in the more solid branches of an English education. If a girl begins to get interested in the school work, and is seen in the evening busy over her theme, her mother comes to me and says, ' Now, Miss ——, you must not make Augusta a blue.'"

It would be tedious, even if I had time, to repeat the opinion of each inspector. Suffice it to say that their testimony, and that of the ladies examined before the Commissioners, is unanimous upon the point that the indifference of parents to the education of their daughters, beyond the conventional standard of the society they live in, and the accomplishments which may promote their success in it, is the real stumbling-block in the way of any improvement. This holds good even in the class who receive their education in the national schools.* If we seek for the cause of this indifference, we shall find it in that fatal view of education which regards only its money value, and estimates it solely as a means of "getting on." "The knowledge which will pay in the business or pursuits a lad is likely to enter, is fully appreciated by the parents," says Mr. Fitch; "but the only business of life which they contemplate for their daughters is marriage, and they ask for an education which will fit her for this end. And the accomplishments which they value are those which promise rather to increase her attractiveness before marriage than her happiness or usefulness after that event." I could quote passage after passage to the same effect from these reports, and from every writer on female education, and I appeal to the experience of every one present to confirm the accuracy of the statement. There is a pretty theory abroad, which is always brought forward when women's education is talked about, i.e. that they are educated to be wives and mothers. I do

* See Report of Committee of Council on Education for 1869-70. Mr. Allington's Report, page 28. "Girls fail much more frequently than boys in all subjects and in all standards. It does not necessarily follow that they are inferior to boys in capacity, but as a matter of fact, owing partly to previous neglect and partly to the comparative indifference with which even sensible parents still regard the education of their daughters, the girls in towns and villages, where there are separate departments, are as a rule far below the boys in attainments."

B 2

not know a more fallacious one.* They are *not* educated to be wives, but to get husbands. They are *not* educated to be mothers ; if they were, they would require and obtain the highest education that could be given, in order to fit them for the highest duties a human being can perform. They are *not* educated to be the mistresses of households; if they were, their judgment would be as sedulously trained, habits of method and accuracy as carefully formed, as they are now neglected. They would not give, as Mr. Bryce calculates, 5,520 hours of their school life to music against 640 to arithmetic ; and social and political economy, which are scarcely thought of in their course of instruction now, would take the foremost place in it. What they are educated for is to come up to a certain conventional standard accepted in the class to which they belong, to adorn (if they can) the best parlour or the drawing-room, as it may be, to gratify a mother's vanity, to amuse a father's leisure hours, above all, to get married.†
And here I must mention the cruel result of this fixed idea in men's minds that their daughters are to be provided for by marriage. No other provision is made for them, nor are they trained or allowed to provide for themselves. From the highest ranks of the aristocracy down to the lowest stratum of the middle-class, the rule, which is best

* Appendix XI.   † Appendix XII.

proved by the few exceptions to it, is that no adequate provision, if any, is made for daughters.
£5000, which invested in Consols would produce
£150 per annum, is the ordinary fortune of a peer's
or country gentleman's daughter, who has been
bred up from her cradle in the lap of luxury, and
is probably accustomed to spend that sum upon
her dress.

A solicitor in large practice told a friend of mine
that he had constantly reason, in drawing up wills
and settlements for rich and aristocratic clients, to
ask the question, " Do you intend your daughters
to live in lodgings with one servant ?" Among
the poorer gentry and the professional classes no
provision at all is or can be made for daughters,
and the only thing which might be done for them,
i.e. to train them by education and habits to provide for themselves, is not done or even thought of.
They are brought up to think it a degradation to
gentlewomen to work for their bread, and when
the time comes, as it too surely must come to large
numbers, when they can get no bread but what
they work for, they find themselves as utterly unfitted for the work as they were taught to believe
the work was unfitted for them. The only occupation open to them is the very one for which they
are least prepared, *i.e.* that of a governess, which,
for that reason, is overstocked with incompetent
people; and even that involves some loss of caste.

We hear much of the sanctity of marriage, of

the happiness of domestic life. Is it the best way to preserve them to make the worldly and pecuniary motives for entering upon marriage so strong as to overpower all others? If the girl who sells herself for the comforts or luxuries of life turns out a wife who thinks more of the things she bargained for than the duties she accepted in return, they, at least, have no right to throw a stone at her whose customs reduce her to the alternative of marrying for a provision, or leading a life of poverty, so dull, so narrow, so colourless, so exiled from all she has been taught to value, that only the highest strain of moral courage is equal to accepting it voluntarily. It is easy to laugh at old maids, it is easy to praise them as the sisters of mercy of life, it is not easy to measure the amount of silent suffering, of slow wasting away of hope, of energy, of faculty, as the woman sees her youth passing away, the boundless horizon of earlier years narrowing more and more, middle age finding her as helplessly dependent in her father's house, as unable to gratify a single taste, to follow a single pursuit, which does not chime in with his fancies, as she was at 18, or left alone to struggle, untrained and unarmed, in the fierce battle of life for the very means of living. In the last report of the Society for the Employment of Women, it is state that, according to the census of 1861, there were upwards of three millions of Englishwomen maintaining themselves by their own exertions, a number on which the census of 1871 will probably rather show an increase than a diminution; and allowing that a large per-centage of these belong to the wage-earning classes, there still remains a great proportion who belong to the classes above these. Difficult as it is to find remunerative employment for the daughters of barristers, lawyers, clergymen, and naval and military officers, it is even more difficult to find women in that class fit to do the work when found.

Miss King, the secretary to the society, writes to me:—" I cannot state too strongly my conviction of the necessity of more systematic and methodical training for girls. . . . By far the greater number of those who apply to me for work are over 25 years of age. Many have never held any responsible position at home or elsewhere, nor have had training for anything at all. The saddest cases we have to deal with are those of widows or deserted wives, who are left, with children dependent on them, utterly unprovided for." It may be seen from the last sentence that marriage is not always the provision it is supposed to be.

But it is not even on such grounds as these I ask for a higher education for women. I claim it, as the Bishop of Peterborough did the other day at the meeting for Hitchin College, on the ground that they are human beings, with precisely the same kind of faculties, affections, desires, wants as men, though there may be variations in degree;

that their minds are governed by the same laws, and their characters susceptible of being moulded by the same influences. The only special function allotted by nature to women is motherhood; but, as Miss Davies says in her excellent little book, ' Higher Education of Women,' "the education which produces the best wives and mothers, is likely to be the best possible education. . . . Having made this admission, - it is necessary to point out that an education of which the aim is thus limited, is likely to fail in that aim;" and she goes on to show this by transferring the case to the education of men: . . . " An education which produces the best husbands and fathers is likely to be in all respects the best, because the best man in any capacity must be the man who can measure most accurately the proportion of all his duties and claims, giving to each its due share of his time and energy. A man will not be the better husband and father for neglecting his obligations as a citizen, or as a man of business; nor will a woman be the better wife or mother through ignorance or disregard of other responsibilities."

Let men and women alike, then, be educated as human beings. Here, however, I must guard against the fatal confusion so common in this country, between education and instruction or preparation for the special profession or work of life. It is owing to this confusion that we hear of elementary education, consisting of the " three R's," of the necessity of technical education superseding classical, &c., &c., of women, or of the working classes being enough educated already, and being thus unfitted for the duties of their position. But the true meaning of the word education is not instruction, technical or otherwise. It is intellectual, moral, and physical development, the development of a sound mind in a sound body, the training of reason to form just judgments, the discipline of the will and the affections to obey the supreme law of duty, the kindling and strengthening of the love of knowledge, of beauty, of goodness, till they become governing motives of action. This alone is truly education, to be begun in the first twenty years of life, to be carried on through time, and as I trust, through eternity; and this is the education which should be given, or at any rate aimed at, in the case of every human being. Once accept this view of education, and there is an end of all the distracting talk about this education being good for a man, that for a woman, this for working men, that for tradesmen or professional men, or men of fortune. The technical education may be different for all these, but the education of reason, and conscience, and will, and affections, must be the same for all; and the test to be applied to every proposed system will be this:—Does it tend to form a sound judgment, an enlightened conscience, a disciplined will, a heart loving whatever things are true, honest, just, pure, and lovely?

It would seem scarcely necessary that I should dwell on the social and national importance of the education of women, but the neglect of it would not be so general if that importance were fully recognised. If it be an indisputable axiom that as is the mother so will be the home training, and as is the home training so, in the vast majority of cases, will be the tone of mind and habits which the children take out with them into the world as men and women, then the opinion of Mr. Hare, quoted in the General Report of the Schools Inquiry Commission, to the effect that " an educated mother is of even more importance to the family than an educated father," is fully justified. I could quote passage after passage from these reports, shewing that it is to a higher tone of mind, a wider and more refined culture among the women of the middle class, that we must look to rescue the men from the narrowness of mind, the vulgarity, the absorption of energy and intelligence in money making alone, which threatens to lower the tone of national character, and to make us really what the First Napoleon accused us of being, " a nation of shopkeepers."* In the higher classes, if, as doubtless is the case, the preference of idle and frivolous men for idle and frivolous women tends to keep down the tone of women's education, it is equally certain that the women re-act on the

* Appendix XIII.

men, and the latter will do well to remember Mr. Stuart Mill's eloquent warning to them, that, in the present state of society, if they will not raise women to their level, the women will infallibly drag them down to theirs. Let me, finally, quote the testimony of a man of another country and another form of faith, Monseigneur Dupanloup, Bishop of Orleans, who, some years ago, struck with the evils arising from the deficient education of his countrywomen, wrote a little book entitled " Les Femmes Studieuses." * In that book, after having shown that the education of Christian women, destined to be the companions of men in earthly as in heavenly things, " cannot be too consecutive, too masculine, or too serious," he proceeds to describe what it is, and paints a picture of his countrywomen's ignorance, idleness, and frivolity; of their corrupting influence on society, on their husbands, and their homes, not through vice, but through their narrowmindedness, their incapacity to comprehend any higher aims or feel any large sympathy, their intolerance of any life less idle than their own, which would be painful to read at any time, but is terribly painful now, when read by the light of the last year's events. When that book was written, France stood foremost among the nations, to all appearance great, strong, skilled in all the arts of peace and war.

* Translated into English under the title of " Studious Women," by Mr. Phillimore.

What is she now? In the hour of trial everything failed her—her manhood, her genius, above all, her long boasted military organisation; and when civil war broke out to complete the ruin begun by foreign invasion, the upper and middle classes in Paris, armed and organised though they were, made but one senseless attempt to meet the insurgents, and then fled from the city, and from the homes they should have defended, or silently submitted to the tyranny of the minority they hated and despised. Looking back to the history of French society for many generations, as painted both in the lighter and more serious literature of France, I hold it not too much to say that one and not the least powerful cause which led to a national collapse, so unprecedented in its swiftness and completeness, may be found in the lowering influence incessantly exercised by the women on the men. What high sense of duty,—that salt of society without which it grows corrupt and worthless,— what noble ideal of patriotism and self-sacrifice, what comprehension even of the issues at stake, could be expected from the sons of such mothers, the husbands of such wives, as are pourtrayed with the intimate knowledge of a father confessor and a man of the world by Bishop Dupanloup?

I think I have made good my assertions respecting the low state of women's education in this country. I turn now to the means of raising it from this condition, and to the main object which I had in view in bringing the subject before you, *i.e.*, the hope that this Society, which has already done so much for education, will take the matter up, and lend its powerful aid to the scheme I have to propose. There is, fortunately, almost complete unanimity of opinion amongst those who have most fully considered the subject, as to the remedies required. They are:—

1. The creation of a sounder public opinion respecting the need and obligation of educating girls.

2. The re-distribution of educational endowments, so as to give a fair share of them to girls.

3. The improvement of female teachers by their examination and registration according to fixed standards.

Allow me to say a few words on each of these points, and, first, as to the creation of a sounder public opinion respecting the education of girls.

I have already laid before you a mass of evidence to prove that the great hindrance to improvement in girls' education is the total indifference to it of parents; an indifference bred by the tone of society which neither requires nor values in women the results of a good education; and the more than indifference, the very common dislike among men, young men especially, to a high standard of education for women. So long as parents look to marriage as the one provision for their daughters, the *summum bonum* to be obtained for them, so long will women's education be adapted solely to please what are called marrying men. No woman can be more convinced than I am that a happy marriage is the *summum bonum* of a woman's life, but so it seems to me it is equally of a man's, and surely to the woman as the man it should not be an object to be striven for, but to be received as the supreme grace of fate when the right time and the right person come.

The reform of public opinion on this point would ensure every other reform. If ever it be possible to make cultivation, knowledge, and serious work the fashion for women, the battle would be virtually won. I remember at the time when all the feminine world walked in gigantic crinolines, that an examination of a National Girls' School, in a somewhat remote country district, showed forty of the girls to have crinolines and only one a pocket-handkerchief. That is about the proportion now between the girls who have a smattering of accomplishments and those who are really educated. Is it too Utopian to hope that a day may come when the proportion shall be reversed, and when it will be considered as disgraceful for a woman to be without preparation for the serious work of life as it would be now for any one above the gutter to be without a pocket-handkerchief ?

With regard to the second remedy, the extension of endowments to girls, opinion is equally unanimous among all the authorities I have consulted. The necessity of institutions for girls, holding the same place in their education, as grammar schools, public schools, and the universities do in that of boys, is strongly insisted upon by the assistant commissioners in these reports.*

Mr. Green says:—" The education of boys in England has only been saved from the abyss of triviality and vulgarity by the application, however clumsy, of endowments. For girls the same salvation can only be obtained in the same way." And Mr. Bryce places first among the remedies from the application of which an improvement in the education of girls may be hoped for, the establishment of schools for girls under public authority and supervision. Hitherto, however, the claims of girls have been almost entirely disregarded; the Schools Inquiry Commissioners state that it is evident that the endowments for the secondary education of girls bear but an infinitesimal proportion to the similar endowments for boys. They go on to say, " It is certainly a singular fact, and one not by any means admitting of easy explanation, that, with these few exceptions, no part of the large funds arising from endowments, and applicable to educational objects for the upper and middle classes, is now, or has been for a long time past, devoted to so important a purpose as the education

* Appendix XIV.

of girls and young women." The fact seems
scarcely so singular to women, to whom the difficulty of obtaining funds for any scheme destined
to benefit them is but too familiar. The same
difficulty of obtaining money for the better education of women stands in the way of the Hitchin
College, the only institution yet offering to women
the greatly needed and greatly desired advantages
of a university education, and also of the North
London Collegiate Schools, founded by the public
spirit and self-sacrificing generosity of the principal, Miss Buss, whose noble act in endowing the
schools has met with no adequate response. "It
is a noteworthy fact," says Mr. Fitch, in a note
appended to his report, "that in the city of
London a new trust fund of more than £60,000 has
just been created for improving the education of
boys, notwithstanding the existence of enormous
unused endowments for precisely the same purpose. No part of this is available for girls. Mer-
chants and bankers subscribe freely; even a joint-
stock company contributes £1000, on the express
ground that a better race of clerks and "commercial" men is wanted to do the work of the City.
But for those who are to be the wives of these
men, whose influence will determine the characters
which they form, and the lives they lead, no provision is even contemplated."

The last of these words are no longer true.
Mr. Rogers is contemplating making a provision

for the middle class girls of London; but as I understand that he can only get shillings for the girls where he got pounds for the boys, and has been unable yet to raise for them one-twentieth of the sum which was subscribed at once for their brothers, the scheme has not yet been carried into effect.*

* Mr. (Rev. W.) Rogers, who was chairman of the meeting, in tendering the vote of thanks to Mrs. Grey, said he could not quite agree with one statement she had put forward, viz. that there was no demand on the part of parents for a higher kind of education: on the contrary, there was a widespread dissatisfaction with the present state of things. Being anxious to establish a girls' school in connection with the Boys' Middle Class School in London, they sent round a paper to the parents of the boys—who numbered about 1,100—asking their opinion, and they received answers and promises that the girls should be sent, if the school were opened, from about 500. He regretted he had not brought any of the answers which had been received, but they were very remarkable, as showing how very unfortunate many of the parents had been in trying to obtain a good education for their girls. It was not quite true that where pounds were subscribed for the boys' school there was a difficulty in getting shillings for the girls, for he believed the necessary funds would be forthcoming, but the real difficulty was in finding a suitable site, and also in getting good teachers. It was felt that a girls' school must be placed in a different kind of locality to that which would do for a boys' school, but he was now in a position to say that he believed one had been chosen, and that before long the school would be open. He should be sorry for the idea to get abroad that gentlemen in London were not as anxious for the education of girls as of boys; it was not money which caused the delay, but a feeling of delicacy, and the desire that the thing should be done in a proper manner.

C

It is some comfort to find this matter thus strongly summed up in the Commissioners' Report: —" We conceive that, even were the bearing of the old deeds far more manifest than it is, the exclusion of girls from the benefit of educational endowments would be in the highest degree inexpedient and unjust; and we cannot believe, that in any comprehensive adjustment of these great questions, it will be defended or maintained."

It is cheering also to find that there is a disposition among the more enlightened of the community, including the Endowed Schools Commissioners themselves, to redress this grievance. Lord Lyttelton, in his speech at the meeting in behalf of Hitchin College, invited pressure from without, as being the best help that could be given to the Commissioners towards carrying into practical effect their good intentions in this respect. It is such a pressure that I hope to see exercised by the Educational Association I want your help to form; a pressure, which, I trust, will not be relaxed till we have obtained for girls as well as boys Professor Huxley's ladder from the gutter to the Universities, the steps of the ladder being precisely the same for both. There is much and very weighty evidence to show that it would be an advantage to both sexes, morally and intellectually, as well as an immense saving of money and teaching power, that they should climb it together from the infant school to college inclusive, learning by this common work for common aims to recognise their common human nature, to complement what in each is deficient, and thus to become the true help-mates which God created them to be. The time, however, may not be ripe for this yet. More experience of the working of mixed education may be required before any decisive steps can be taken towards promoting it. But the question of giving to girls their fair share of endowments is ripe for decision, and not a moment should be lost in bringing to bear upon it the utmost available force.

The third remedy I would urge will perhaps meet with readier acceptance than the former, *i.e.*, a system for the examination and registration of teachers according to fixed standards, which should create a body of teachers for secondary schools analogous to the certificated mistresses of elementary schools. I have not time to place before you the evidence I have collected from this book and other sources respecting the miserable incompetency of women teachers as a class, and it appears to me that the results of the teaching in girls' schools, as exhibited in these reports, are sufficient to establish the fact.* Here, again, the larger portion of the blame should be laid on the system, not on the individuals. So long as public opinion decrees that the only genteel occupation

* Appendix XV.

c 2

for women shall be that of a governess, while it decrees also that it is ungenteel to take it up as a profession and prepare for it by thorough training, so long will its ranks be overcrowded with utterly incompetent persons, and the social status and emoluments of female teachers remain at their present low ebb. But with the growing demand for a better education for women there must be necessarily a growing demand for better teachers, and for some means of distinguishing the competent from the incompetent. This would be secured by the registration of teachers according to qualifications, tested either by the local examinations of the Universities or by the College of Preceptors,—whose examinations are open to female as to male teachers,—or by any other body duly appointed for the purpose. It may be that public opinion is not prepared to follow in this country to its full extent the system of Prussia, where no person can teach anything professionally without a certificate of competency from the authorities established under government for that purpose, but the nearer approach that can be made to it, by enlightening the public mind on the necessity of requiring some test of teaching capabilities, and by inducing those who intend to teach to qualify themselves to pass such a test, the better chance there will be of weeding out the present incompetent race of governesses, and replacing them by others trained to their work.

In this, as in the other directions I have indicated, much has been and is being done by the associations in London as also in the provinces, especially the north and west of England.* The University Local Examinations have done much to raise the quality of female education, by giving schools and teachers a standard to work up to. The Hitchin College carries the standard up to the point of a Cambridge degree. The courses of lectures for women provided in London and in the North of England, though they are, as Mr. Fitch said the other day, to be looked upon rather as stimulants than food, and can by no means take the place of thorough teaching, have stirred up an interest and created a desire for knowledge unknown before. Good and zealous work is going on, and beginning to bear fruit. But these efforts are little known or felt by the general public, and what I believe is still wanted, is some general organisation that should draw into union and co-operation all these separate movements, and give to them the strength which belongs to combined and systematic action.

This, then, is the scheme to which I trust this Society will lend its aid, *i.e.* to form an Educational Association, embracing all those who are actively interested in the cause, and having for its object to carry what I may call the three points of the educational charter of women:—

1. The equal right of women to the education recognised as the best for human beings.

* Appendix XVI.

2. The equal right of girls to a share in the existing educational endowments of the country, and to be considered, no less than boys, in the creation of any new endowments.

3. The registration of teachers, with such other measures as may raise teaching to a profession as honourable and honoured for women as for men.

Such an Association might be represented in London by a central committee, connected with local committees formed in every considerable country town. By common action from all these different centres, a body of evidence might be collected on every point connected with the better education of girls of all classes, which would be of invaluable service in guiding the action both of school boards, and of the Endowed Schools Commissioners, as of all other bodies and individuals concerned; and by means of lectures, meetings, journalism, and social influence, an agitation might be set on foot and kept up active enough and penetrating enough to reach even the subsoil of the British mind, and to force upon it, not only the recognition of the fact which it now, according to Mr. Bryce, holds to be an obnoxious and revolutionary paradox, "That the minds of women are as cultivable, and as well worth cultivating as those of men," but that it is of vital national importance that the minds of those who exercise such an enormous though indirect influence on the destinies of the nation, should be cultivated to the full measure of their capabilities.

Since I first conceived this scheme, I have received assurances of sympathy and co-operation from many who may be considered as representative men and women, and whose names would be a sufficient pledge to the public for the character of the undertaking. I believe that I could have obtained many more if I had not been so heavily pressed for time; and I have no doubt that, should such an Association as I have proposed be formed, it will soon number among its members most of those whose co-operation would be of any value.

I now leave the matter in your hands, and have only to thank you very earnestly for giving me this opportunity of laying it before you.

APPENDIX I.*

Constitution of Royal Commission.

" In the year 1864, a Royal Commission was issued for enquiring into the education given in schools not included in former Commissions, and also for ' considering and reporting what measures, if any, were required for the improvement of such education, having especial regard to all endowments applicable, or which can rightly be made applicable thereto.' The members were as follows :—Lord Taunton, Lord Stanley, Lord Lyttelton, Sir Stafford Northcote, The Dean of Chichester, Dr. Temple, the Rev. Anthony Thorold, Mr. Acland, Mr. Baines, Mr. Forster, Mr. Erle, and Dr. Storrer. These Commissioners appointed Assistant Commissioners, and assigned to them certain districts as follows :—

London, embracing a circle of 12 miles radius from Charing Cross :—D. R. Fearon, M.A., Her Majesty's Inspector of Schools.

Surrey (outside the London Postal District) and Sussex :—H. A. Giffard, M.A., Sen. Student, Christ Church, Oxford.

Devon and Somerset, with Bristol and its suburbs :—C. H. Stanton, M.A., Barrister.

Stafford and Warwickshire :—T. H. Green, Fellow of Balliol College, Oxford.

Norfolk, Northumberland, and several towns :—J. L. Hammond, M.A., Fellow of Trinity College, Cambridge.

York and West Riding :—J. G. Fitch, M.A., Her Majesty's Inspector of Schools.

Lancashire and Birkenhead :—J. Bryce, B.C.L., Fellow of Oriel College, Oxford.

---

* Throughout the Appendix, the references, when it is not otherwise stated, are to the volume of Reports on the Education of Girls, edited by Miss Beale.

Flint, Denbigh, Montgomery, Glamorgan, and Hereford-shire, with Shrewsbury and Monmouth:—H. M. Bompas, M.A., Cambridge and London, Barrister.

No schools out of the districts were visited, but the Principals of some important schools beyond these limits were requested to give evidence before the Commissioners in London."—*Preface to Reports*, p. vi.

APPENDIX II.

" A glance at the contents of such a book as 'Mangnall's Questions' will explain the essential difference between the means adopted for the mental culture of boys and girls after the age of fifteen. If it did not originally determine, it has done much to perpetuate the conditions, now considered most essential for the intellectual training of young ladies. . . . The historical and biographical portions occupy about 450 pages, and traverse the whole area of history from the accepted date of the deluge. . . . A girl, whose only notions of ancient history is likely to be derived from this source, gets confused by a multitude of names which have for her no individual reality or interest. Again, in books of this, and even of a far better stamp, there is no opportunity of discussing the degree of credibility due to each historic period. Everything recorded, be it myth or fact, is treated with the same consideration and respect. One lady, indeed, preferred the Assyrian and Babylonian monarchies as the most interesting of all eras; and her mode of questioning shewed that she did not regard the investigation of facts as a matter of any importance. Dates were asked for in the most random order.* Cæsar's invasion of Britain slipping in between the Deluge and the Siege of Troy. . . . What is chiefly to be regretted is

---

* The same peculiarity is observable in " Eve's Questions," a book much used in Ladies' Schools.

that at an age when an intelligent young woman might be initiated in a course of rational and laborious study, so as ultimately to acquire a taste for critical research, and an insight into the philosophy of the subject, her time and energies should be frittered away upon a miscellaneous collection of small facts, legendary, historical, biographical, astronomical, scientific, and general, all useful to know, but yet incapable of being combined and organised into a means of strengthening and hardening the intellect.

The following are taken at random from the performances of various scholars at different schools. They are transcribed *literatim*, and it would have been easy, but tedious, to add to the collection :—

" Lord Bacon—Henry III—He discovered a great many " things in chemistry and discovered gunpowder."

" Lord Bacon was a celebrated philosopher and he invented " gunpowder."

" Sir Thomas Moore. Lord Chancellor of England. Wrote " plays and lived in Henry VIII. reign."

" Sir Thomas Moore—A poet in the reign of Victoria."

" Burke a navigator.

" Sir I. Newton—George IV—Astronomer."

" Dr. Johnson one of the brightest luminaries of the 18th " century."

" Sir W. Scott—flourished in the reign of Elizabeth."

" Milton, was a celebrated poet. His best poem is Pardise " lost and regained."

The same inspector says that " in geography the chief fault " was in the spelling of names and places," and subjoins a few specimens taken at random :—

" Britian—Nolfolk—Chatam—Corsicia—Sibraria—Calafor- " nia—Amarica." One girl wrote Oder and Elbe in one word —" Orderandable." There were not a few answers of the following kind—" We obtain cotton from Scotland."—*Report of Mr. Hammond*, pp. 140-44.

APPENDIX III.

" It is incredible how many girls from nearly every school write down such answers as the following. 'How do nouns substantive form their plural number?' 'Sometimes by changing a vowel, as, ox, oxen.'

" To the question, How is the past tense of verbs formed? I have received a vast number of answers, more or less like this one. 'By adding d or ed, as, sing, sang.' Few ever mention what the affix is added to. One girl answers the same question simply thus ; ' more, most.' "—*Report of Mr. Hammond*, page 140.

" A boy who learns Latin, even in a clumsy way, is forced to attend to grammar, *per se*, and learns, however dimly, that there are laws in human speech, and principles which underlie the structure of words and sentences. But there is nothing analogous to this in girls' schools."—*Report of Mr. Fitch*, page 35.

APPENDIX IV.

" In all the girls' schools where it was possible to do so, I set an examination paper in arithmetic, giving to the more advanced classes the same questions as were given to the less advanced classes in the boys' schools of the same social rank. With a few brilliant exceptions, the results were most unsatisfactory."—*Report of Mr. Bryce*, p. 56.

" One of the best managed large private schools of the second grade sent in thirteen senior pupils to the first examination conducted by the Cambridge syndicate. At Christmas, 1863, of these thirteen only three passed, eight having failed entirely in arithmetic, and that subject only."—*Report of Mr. Fearon,* p. 91.

" I have fifty-two examination papers, written by pupils who have entered above the age of fifteen. An analysis of the papers gives the following results:—

" Fractions . . . . . . 8, each sum set was wrong.
Rule of Three or Practice 18, each sum wrong.
Compound Long Division 14, of these 13 were wrong.
Compound Short Division 1, wrong.
Compound Multiplication 5, all wrong.
Simple Multiplication . 3, 2 right."—*Evidence of Miss Beale, Principal of Cheltenham College for Ladies,* p. 197.

" The papers of the Alnwick girls were the worst I have ever seen. Out of forty-six sums, only five were perfectly satisfactory, and thirty-nine were utterly worthless. A simple question in notation elicited one correct and eight incorrect answers, and the latter differed from one another by trillions. The Berwick girls passed a creditable examination, and proved themselves to be decidedly superior to the boys at the same school.

" It was remarked to me in Northumberland, that the reason why women were not more frequently employed in shops and offices was because of their inaptitude for figures."—*Report of Mr. Hammond,* page 138, note.

APPENDIX V.

" It would not be admitted by teachers that science is absent from their curriculum. ' My young people,' said one lady to me, ' take great interest in science. We have a lecturer who comes weekly during the season, and gives us courses on astronomy, heraldry, botany, and architecture. Sometimes too, when it is fine, they go out and pluck flowers, and afterwards dissect them, and have a lesson on their parts.' I found on inquiry, that this arrangement prevailed at several schools in the district; and there are two or three gentlemen of real ability and good local reputation, who itinerate among the Ladies' Schools to give lectures of this kind. . . . In lectures of this sort there is little or no teaching: they bear no relation to the studies pursued in the interval; they are supplemented by no regular reading; they are tested by no examinations. The day of lecture, is, however, looked forward to as an event; other lessons are put away; dress is especially attended to; and the young ladies, ranged in close order, sit and smile rather as spectators at a festal exhibition than as students: here and there it may be hoped that some pupil is interested and encouraged to pursue the subject farther; but I can not express my sense of the uselessness of such displays to average pupils, nor of the meretricious character of a course of instruction which professes to explain heraldry, architecture, or botany, to young girls of 13 or 14 in six lectures."—*Report of Mr. Fitch*, page 36, 37.

APPENDIX VI.

The following are some specimens of translation of a passage of Macaulay's History into French, by a large first class in a remarkably well conducted private school of the first grade, and Mr. Fearon considers them not unfavourable specimens of the character of the work done in French in these schools. The sentence: "Charles, however, had one advan-
" tage, which, if he had used it well, would have more than
" compensated for the want of stores and money, and which,
" notwithstanding his mismanagement, gave him, during some

" months, a superiority in the war," is translated thus by Number 27 :—

" Charles avait, cependant, un avantage, lequel, s'il avait " servi bien, aurait plus compensé pour le besoin de stores et de " monnaie : et lequel, néan moins son mal-management, donna " lui, pendant quelques mois une superiorité dans le guerre."

Number 15 writes : " que lui donné un superiorite dans la " guerre. Ses troupes, en premier, batturent beaucoup meillures " que ces du parlement."

Number 22 translates, " in spite of his mismanagement," " Malgré de son deshabille."

Number 12 renders : " The parliamentary ranks were filled " with hirelings, whom want and idleness had induced to en- " list," " Ses ranks parlementaires étaient remplis d'hommes " qui la necessité et la paresse avait pérsuadérent à enlister."

The words : " And even Hampden's regiment was described " by Cromwell as a mere rabble of tapsters and serving-men " out of place," are thus rendered by Number 28 : " Et même " ce regiment fut ecrit par Cromwell comme une collection " d'hommes brusques et domestiques mal apropos."

Nor are the results of the translations from French into English much more satisfactory. " Even in the best private schools they cannot be called *good*. The translations in these schools which are not among the best are really deplorable. On one occasion . . . I gave them a short and very simple passage which they had read to translate upon paper, and found that some of them did not know the English of the most com- mon words or the meaning of the most ordinary expression. For example, (p. 101) the words, ' L'hotesse dormait dans un coin de la cuisine,' were rendered by one pupil (aged 16) ' The hostess slept in a (blank) with the cook.' By another (aged 22), ' The hostess slept in a (blank) with her cousin.' "—*Report of Mr. Fearon*, page 99.

APPENDIX VII.

"Music not only engrosses an exorbitant share of time and labour, but is so managed as to secure the maximum of injury to other subjects of study. For as practising goes on all day long, and as there are few pianos and many girls, each has to leave the class in which she may happen to be when her turn for practising comes, or when the music or singing master arrives to give his lesson."—*Report of Mr. Bryce*, p. 53.

"After examining a great number of time tables, I found reason to believe that, taking the number one to represent the total quantity of working time at a girl's disposal, (*i.e.* about from 36 to 40 hours per week) the time spent upon each subject in the more expensive Ladies' Schools might be approximately stated as follows : —

Subject.	*Time Spent.*
Music	·25
Miscellaneous information	·15
French	·12
History	·08
Drawing	·065
Arithmetic	·075
German	·045
Geography	·05
Writing	·06
English Grammar	·045
Use of Globes	·025
Needlework	·035
	1·000

It will be noticed that of the whole available time of a school girl, one fourth is spent upon music, and one thirteenth only upon arithmetic. If we were to divide the subjects of instruction into three classes, those which rank as accomplishments, those in which facts only are taught and little or no intellectual training given, and those whose study almost necessarily involves some healthy mental effort, such as arithmetic, English grammar, French, and German, we should find that subjects of the first class occupied considerably more than one-third of a girl's school life, these of the second class about one-third, those of the last class not much more than one-fourth."—*Report of Mr. Bryce*, p. 54.

" As regards the teaching of music in these schools, I am inclined to infer :

(*a.*) That sufficient attention is not generally paid to accurate and careful instruction in harmony and that which may be called the grammar of music.

(*b.*) That much money is spent on the teaching of instrumental music by expensive masters to girls who have not sufficient correctness of ear (or are otherwise unqualified) to play in such a style as to interest themselves, or avoid torturing their friends. When these girls marry they drop their playing altogether.

(*c.*) That even in cases where pupils have sufficient taste to make it worth their while to cultivate instrumental music, that taste is often not judiciously directed. They are allowed to play trashy but showy music, and are not required to study classical compositions with sufficient care and assiduity."—*Report of Mr. Fearon*, p. 103.

" The time wasted on this accomplishment is deplorable. I was assured by many mistresses that at least one quarter to one third of those who devoted hours to its acquisition, when they left school, never again opened a piano ; and surely it would seem that when a girl showed a marked disinclination for it, some more profitable study might be substituted."—*Report of Mr. Stanton*, p. 115.

APPENDIX VIII.

A.

Unsatisfactory State of Education in First Grade Schools.

" On the whole, the conclusion to which, at the close of my inquiry into the condition of these first grade schools, I have come is, that the results of the education given in them are by no means satisfactory. I have already in the course of this Report, either stated or alluded to the principal causes of this unsatisfactory condition of things. But I may, perhaps, be permitted to collect in this place, and briefly recapitulate these causes. They are :—

" (*a*.) The multiplicity of subjects of which it is thought necessary that a girl should know something. The consequent distraction of mind, and want of thoroughness in any important subject. Subordinately, the time given to showy accomplishments to the exclusion of sound learning.

" (*b*.) The want of continuity, regularity, and system in the education of girls. The removing of them from one school to another, and again to home or to the houses of friends and relations on long visits. Their consequent imperfect grounding in elementary subjects.

" (*c*.) The want of systematic and well-directed physical education for girls; which, coupled with the fitful character of their mental education, is often the cause of failures of health, and which renders them less able to study successfully than they would otherwise be.

" (*d*.) The want of a stimulus to the girls when they are at school. The fact that none of the schools, not even the public schools, have any systematic independent examinations. More important still, the fact that there is no provision for the higher education of women, and consequently no superior body which can set the standard of education for the schools, or give point and aim to the work done in them.   No goal for the education of girls.

" (e.) The want of higher education, cultivation, and information in the governesses who teach in these schools. Akin to this, the low salaries given to them.

" (f.) The want, also, among them, of knowledge of the art of teaching."—*Mr. Fearon's Report*, pp. 103, 104.

B.

Chief Defects in the Education of Women.

" 1. The Schools are too numerous and too small.   Such competition as there is among them is a competition which lowers the price of education, but does not improve its quality.

" 2. There is no external stimulus to a School, and no test of the quality of its teaching.   The same is true of the great majority of the private adventure Boys' Schools, especially the cheap ones, and it is one of the causes of their low estate.   . . In the case of girls, even that slight test is wanting which is supposed to be furnished to the cheaper Boys' Schools, by the fitness of the pupils for mercantile situations.

" 3. The teaching of almost all Girls' Schools, both dear and cheap, wants thoroughness. This is due to three causes :—

" (a.) The subjects which custom has fixed are not subjects which encourage and require a thorough manner of treatment.   Of course any subject, even heraldry or worsted-work, is learnt more profitably when it is learnt thoroughly.   But the need of thoroughness and of the constant exercise of the intelligence as well as the memory is more violently forced upon the teacher's mind in working at arithmetic, mathematics, and Latin, than in running through manuals of history, geography, and general knowledge.

" Unfortunately arithmetic, mathematics, and Latin, are the three subjects most neglected in Girls' Schools. French and German might in some degree replace Latin, but French and German are usually committed to unscientific hands, and dealt with in a superficial way.

" (b.) Too many subjects are taught at once, and each of them is taught intermittently.

" (c.) The teaching wants a practical aim. It is for show and not for use, for seeming and not for being.

" 4. Early education is very generally neglected.

" 5. There is an insufficient supply of competent teachers."
—*Report of Mr. Bryce*, pp. 78, 79.

APPENDIX IX.

Digest of Evidence given before the Schools Inquiry Commission.

As far as the great essentials are concerned, the education of girls is extremely inferior ; a very undue proportion of their time is spent in accomplishments.—*Albert Creak, Esq., M.A., M.C.P. Blue Book*, Vol. v. p. 191.

Education of girls more defective than boys.—*T. Torr, Esq., Aylesbury Manor, Lincolnshire, Farmer, Schools Inquiry Commission.* Vol. ii. *Digest*, p. 88.

The education at present given to girls is imperfect, certainly.—Vol. ii. *Digest*, p. 30; *Mr. E. Edmunds, Rugby.*

There is a great want of good education for girls in the middle rank of life.—*The Rev. C. Evans, M.A.* Vol. iv. p. 563.

In private schools a very inferior instruction is obtained.—*The Rev. R. Gregory.* Vol. v. p. 618.

The general state of their education is very unfortunate.—*W. B. Hodgson, LL.D., Vice-President of the College of Preceptors*, Vol. ii. *Digest*, p. 47.

Girls are almost universally less well educated than their brothers.—*Gertrude King, Secretary of the Society for the Promotion of Employment for Women.* Vol. ii. p. 52.

The means of education for girls of the middle classes are very bad, and still more deficient than those for boys; the chief thing is that at present their instruction is so exceedingly unsystematic.—*R. R. W. Lingen, Esq.* Vol. ii. *Digest*, p. 55.

Deficiency in education of daughters of professional men; at the present time they are educated mainly by governesses, a few by select boarding-schools, and many of them take their chance at home, and get masters. The girls of the middle classes are necessarily worse educated than their brothers, because the brothers have at least learned that occupation in which they are to earn their bread, whereas the girls have not even learned that. A serious defect in female education is the routine way which governesses have in teaching arithmetic.—*The Rev. Mark Pattison, B.D., Rector of Lincoln College, Oxford.* Vol. ii. *Digest*, p. 66.

The standard for the education of girls is lower than it ought to be, which is attributable to defective teaching.—*Miss M. Porter.* Vol. ii. *Digest*, p. 70.

The education of girls in the upper middle class is very unsatisfactory, the chief defect being the want of thorough teaching; the education of girls in the lower middle class is worse still, and below that of boys in the same condition of life. The great defect in girls' education is its deficient character.—*Miss M. E. Smith, Visitor of Bedford College.* Vol. ii. *Digest*, p. 82.

Girls suffer from the absolute want of anything like an accurate foundation for their education; there is a good deal of accuracy attempted in finishing, as, for instance, in French, there is a great effort made to teach girls to speak and write the language, but there is no grammatical knowledge, nothing upon which that further knowledge can be safely built.—*The Rev. F. V. Thornton, M.A., Rector of Callington, Cornwall.* Vol. ii. *Digest*, p. 86.

There is as great a want of schools for girls of the class that would be above going to a national school as for boys.—

The Rev. H. Twells, M.A., Head Master of the Godolphin School, Hammersmith. Vol. ii. *Digest,* p. 90.

The education of girls has some of the same defects as that of boys, they are taught by rote rather than by thought : the teaching is made the practice of memory rather than the practice of intellectual power.—*O. C. Waterfield, Esq., M.A., Head Master of a Private School at Sheen.* Vol. ii. *Digest,* p. 93.

Education of girls greatly needs improvement.—*The Right Hon. Earl Fortescue.* Vol. ii. *Digest,* p. 35.

APPENDIX X.

26, *Lowndes Square, London, S.W.*
15th *of May,* 1871.

DEAR MRS. GREY,

Every teacher appointed to a school under the Poor Law Board must undergo an examination, and in this way I have come to know the sort of education which many of these women who apply for these situations have received.

The examination is extremely slight, not consisting of more, unless the candidate especially asks it, than a paper containing some elementary questions on Scripture and another paper on arithmetic. The paper contains nine questions on each of these two subjects, and the candidate is required to answer three questions out of each of these nine questions. The questions are not at all more difficult than could be readily answered by any pupil in the first class of an ordinary village school. A first class in a really good village school would go far beyond them.

You will observe that these examinations test the examinee's writing, spelling, knowledge of Bible history, power of composition, and arithmetic. The papers are sometimes so bad that we are only justified in passing the writers at all, by the consideration that if we do not accept them, we should get no candidates for the places at all. The candidates are always respectable women of the middle class, and have sometimes been governesses in private families. Yet their writing is often hardly intelligible, and deformed with such mistakes in spelling as would pluck them in any examination for the lowest Civil Service examination. Their Biblical knowledge is excessively meagre, and their arithmetic worst of all, generally not going further than the simple rules; and if they try a sum in multiplication of money, the working commonly shows fatal blunders. Sometimes seeing that candidates know nothing of these elementary branches of education, I have asked what they do know, and what they have been accustomed to teach in private families. The answer is crochet, the piano, French, Italian; of course it is obvious that their knowledge of all these subjects must be extremely limited.

Believe me, yours sincerely,
E. CARLETON TUFNELL.

APPENDIX XI.

" I cannot find that any part of the training given in ladies' schools educates them for domestic life, or prepares them for duties which are supposed to be especially womanly. I am repeatedly told that cooking, the government of servants, the superintendence of their work, the right management of the purse, and the power to economise all the resources of a household, are of more importance to a girl than learning. All this is confessedly true. But then these things are not taught in schools. Nor are the laws of health, the elements of chemistry, the physiology which would be helpful in the case of children, the political economy which would preserve ladies from mistakes in dealing with the poor; nor any, in short, of those studies which seem to stand in a close relation to the work a woman has to do in the world. Every where the fact, that the pupil is to become a woman and not a man, operates upon her course of study negatively not positively.

It deprives her of the kind of teaching which boys have, but it gives her little or nothing in exchange. It certainly does not give to her any exceptional teaching adapted to her career as a woman."—*Report of Mr. Fitch*, p. 31.

APPENDIX XII.

" After all, the great hindrance to improvement in ladies' schools lies in the very general indifference on the part of parents to the mental cultivation of their daughters. As a rule, the governesses have an ideal of education far higher than that of the average parents, and I have seen many who are earnestly striving to improve the quality of the instruction under the great difficulties of parental apathy or discouragement. Everywhere I am told by governesses that parents cannot ' see the use of' any subject of instruction except plain rudiments and accomplishments."—*Report of Mr. Fitch*, p. 43.

" At present the majority of parents are neither willing to afford the time nor the money necessary to give a real education to their daughters. They are not highly educated themselves, and thinking that marriage is the great market for which all women should prepare themselves, are indifferent to their intellectual progress."—*Report of Mr. Stanton*, p. 116.

Miss Frances Buss told me she considered Miss Garrett's marriage a most fortunate event for the cause of the better education and serious occupation of girls as it would allay the fears of so many mothers that their daughters if highly educated and still more if engaged in professional pursuits would never find husbands."—*M. G. G.*

APPENDIX XIII.

" If one looks to the enormous number of unmarried women in the middle class, who have to earn their bread, at the great drain of the male population of this country for the army, for

India, and for the Colonies, at the expensiveness of living here, and consequent lateness of marriage, it seems to me that the instruction of the girls of a middle class family, for any one who thinks much of it, is important to the very last degree."—*R. R. W. Lingen, Esq., Secretary to Committee of Council on Education. Quoted in Gen. Report*, p. 1.

Mr. Fraser quotes a weighty opinion of Tocqueville, that the chief cause of the prosperity of the United States is the superiority of their women.

The popular feeling to which we have referred, on one most important subject, that of the married life of women, is founded on a grave and radical misconception, a misconception especially, though by no means only, injurious to the middle class, and increasingly so in these days. The most material service may be rendered to the husband, in the conduct of his business and the most serious branches of his domestic affairs, by a wife trained and habituated to a life altogether different from that of mere gentleness and amiability of which we have spoken: a life of no slight intellectual proficiency, and capacity for many functions too commonly thought to be reserved for the male sex.—*General Report of the Schools Inquiry Commissioners*, p. 1.

It is wonderful to see the assumption that the repose and enjoyment of home are in some way incompatible with a loftier standard of intellectual education for women. It is true that no one seems able to point to any example in illustration of the doctrine, or to assert that when we ascend into the households in which the highest feminine culture prevails we find any lack of grace or of affection, any less regard for children, or any disposition to neglect household duties. But it would not be difficult to point to thousands of instances of men who have started in life with a love of knowledge and with a determination to master at least some department of honourable thought or inquiry; yet who have gradually sunk into habits of mental indolence, have allowed all their great aims to fade out of view, and have become content with the reading supplied by Mudie and the newspapers, simply from a dread of isolation, and because these resources sufficed for the intellectual aliment of the rest of the household. There is no hope for the middle classes, until the range of topics which they care about includes something more than money making, religious controversies, and ephemeral politics; nor until they consider that mental cultivation apart from its bearing on the business of life is a high and religious duty.

When they come to consider this, they will set as great a value on intellectual power or literary taste when they are put forth by a girl as by a boy; and they will feel that the true measure of a woman's right to knowledge is her capacity for receiving it, and not any theories of ours, as to what she is fit for or what use she is likely to make of it.—*Report of Mr. Fitch*, p. 43.

The improvement of English schools means nothing less than the elevation of the English commercial class to a higher level of knowledge, taste, and culture, than that at which they now stand. In approaching so great a task as this it may well be thought, there is surely no agency from which more may be hoped than the influence of cultivated women—women who have received from their education, a sounder knowledge than education now gives them, powers of mind more thoroughly trained, a higher conception of the duties which the welfare of society requires them to discharge.— *Report of Mr. Bryce*, p. 83.

APPENDIX XIV.

" *What is wanted is endowment; to induce the girls in second grade schools to continue a course of sound, as opposed to fashionable, instruction, and to furnish the first grade schools with a supply of well grounded pupils.*"—Report of Mr. Fearon, p. 105.

" An instance of what may be achieved in the way of English

education for girls by the good organization, which an endowment makes it possible to maintain, is afforded by the ' Bath Row Elementary School' at Birmingham. The elementary schools on King Edward's foundation for girls, as for boys, have not hitherto generally attempted an education superior in kind to that given in a National School. In the one mentioned, however, I found an upper class of twenty-five girls, who had reached a distinctly higher level. In what is ordinarily understood by ' English education,' they were for their age, better than the best in the ' boarding schools for young ladies,' that I examined, and they had a sound elementary knowledge of French besides. In arithmetic they were simply perfect. In less than an hour I saw them do eighteen sums in fractions, practice, interest, proportion, decimals, and duodecimals; most of them got all the sums right, and the rest had very few mistakes. They did very well in the ' analysis ' of the first book of the Paradise Lost, and would bear pressing in it. The outline of English history they knew thoroughly, and of the other history they were not ignorant: some of them could tell me a good deal, for instance, about the Thirty Years' War. They answered as well as could be wished in geography; French they had not begun long, and had learned quite as a supplementary thing."—*Report of Mr. Green,* p. 159.

" I venture then, in conclusion, to summarize the principal suggestions that seem to arise from the facts and opinions in the foregoing report :—

" 1st. Endowments should be made available for the lower instead of the upper middle classes, especially by providing a good day-school in every town, and cheap boarding-schools for the sons of small farmers.

" 2nd. Opportunities should be offered to all masters and mistresses of having their whole schools examined and reported upon annually by competent examiners.

" 3rd. The subjects and methods of education in girls' schools should be modified.

"4th. Means should be provided for training masters in the art of teaching.

"5th. Examinations should be established or other opportunities afforded to mistresses of proving their proficiency in different branches of knowledge.

"6th. All possible means should be adopted to stir up the parents to take more interest in the education of their children, and to induce them to send their children to school with more regularity."—*Report of Mr. Bompas,* p. 180.

" Have you at all turned your attention to the state of endowments with reference to the schools for girls ?—I feel most strongly, from the people that I have had to do with—professional men with comparatively small incomes—that they can obtain help in the education of their boys, but that no assistance whatever is given in the case of their girls, and that even when willing and able to pay for a good education they cannot get it. There are very many parents who would be glad of some little assistance in the way of a presentation, which makes the payment more easy."—*Evidence of Miss Buss,* p. 215.

" What is your opinion of the general state of the education of the young women of the middle classes of this country ?—I think it is very unfortunate as a rule it is very little what it ought to be, and I regret extremely that in the endowments for education spread over this country at large, the girls have been deprived of their fair share of the benefits that ought to be obtained from that source.

" Do you mean a fair share of those benefits which were intended by the founder ?—I believe in many cases the founders have left the foundations open as regards the sexes, but that the foundations have been appropriated by boys, and that girls have had no benefit from them whatever. Now, if I were made to choose between the two sexes, as was asked just now with reference to classics and physical science, I should say it is more important that girls should be taught even than boys, in this respect, that women are the early trainers of the young, and by the maternal influence the future character is shaped, so that if we had the future mothers of the country well trained there would be an impulse given to the education of boys which from no other quarter can be derived."—*W. B. Hodgson, Esq., LL.D., Evidence before the Schools Inquiry Commissioners.* Vol. v., part 2, p. 1.

"Do you believe there would be any practical obstacles of a formidable nature that would prevent the combination of a system of sound education for girls of the middle classes in every county in England with that of boys under such a system as you have described?—I have always thought that some of the endowments now exclusively applied to boys, or other endowments, as I said before, either nearly useless or worse than useless might, with the greatest advantage be applied to encourage and promote the better education of girls of the middle class."—*Evidence of The Right Hon. Earl Fortescue.* Vol. v. p. 305.

"Have you considered the general question of the interest which girls have in the general endowments for the education of classes above the poor?—Yes, I feel strongly upon that subject."

"What is your opinion on the subject?—I have a very strong feeling that they ought to have a considerable interest in such endowments. I base that opinion on two grounds: 1st, that I do not see why they should be excluded; and 2nd, because my experience as an inspector of schools leads me to say that they would make at least as good a use of them as boys."—*Evidence of the Rev. J. G. C. Fussell, M.A.,* Vol. v. p. 716.

"Have you considered the question of the way in which school endowments are at present applied with reference to the fair claims of women?—I have not considered that question at all. It is simply that I do not understand why endowments should be good for boys, and should necessarily be an evil for girls. I think also that female education needs the help of endowments most, because parents and the public care least about it.

"Many women and amongst them many of those who would best repay the highest culture, are prevented by poverty from getting anything like a complete education."—*Evidence of Miss Wolstenholme.* Vol. v. p, 744

APPENDIX XV.

Defects of Women Teachers.

" Deficient education. This does not usually show itself in gross ignorance, although I am told, and can well believe that such cases are not rare amongst those who teach the cheaper schools; but in an extreme superficiality and flimsiness of knowledge, and in the want of accuracy of mind."—*Report of Mr. Bryce*, p. 67.

"It is certainly true that a very large number of those now engaged in educating girls have never had the slightest special training for it, and have adopted their profession solely because they have no other resource left open to them to obtain a livelihood. In the language of Mr. Bennett, 'Many of them are deficient in mental power and discrimination of character, most of them have mistaken their vocation, and have become teachers when they ought to have been servants.'"—*Report of Mr. Stanton*, p. 117.

"The two capital defects of the teachers of girls, are these: they have not themselves been well taught, and they do not know how to teach. Both these defects are accidental, and may be remedied."—*Report of Mr. Bryce*, p. 169.

"The defects in the teachers seem principally to arise (*a.*) from want of breadth and accuracy of scholarship; (*b.*) from want of knowledge of the art of instructing a class."

"(*a.*) Owing to the entire absence in this country of any public means of superior education for women, of any facilities for their extending their education beyond the age of 17 or 18, there is a lack among them of accurate study and scholarship which must prevail before there can be an abundant supply of women qualified to teach well in first-grade schools."—*Report of Mr. Fearon*, p. 89.

"I have no hesitation in reporting that there are some subjects, those in fact which rest on scientific principles, which females at present cannot teach."—*Report of Mr. Hammond*, p. 150.

Miss Faithful, in the discussion at the Meeting of the Society of Arts, stated that:

"This was a subject which was peculiarly brought home to her, having an office for the employment of women, where she was constantly meeting with applicants of all ages, from 25 to 45, who came to her, saying that they were thrown upon their own resources, that they wanted to do something, that they had no particular bent, but thought they could teach. On being questioned, however, it appeared that they had no knowledge of teaching, and some did not even like it, but there was no other way open to them."

In the discussion which followed the reading of my paper, Mr. Bartley gave the following confirmation of my views :—

"Mr. G. C. T. Bartley said he fully agreed—having made the subject of education his occupation for a long time—with nearly everything said in the paper concerning the deficiency of the education given in girl's schools. He would give an instance of a case which came under his own notice. A little girl, who went to a superior kind of school, was repeating her lessons, and her father caught up the last expression, "Derby, on the Derwent," repeated several times. . . . . . On asking her "What is Derby?" "Oh," said the little girl, "that is not in my lesson." "What is the Derwent?" said the father. "Oh, I was not taught that," said the child ; and there was this little girl positively learning a string of names in that way, without knowing that Derby was a town and that the Derwent was a river."

I may add to this, two anecdotes related to me within these

few days, by two friends of my own. One of them, on showing her little girl some print or picture illustrating an incident in early British history, discovered that neither the child nor the governess knew anything about Caractacus, and the governess, on acknowledging her ignorance, proposed to look for the information in the Encyclopædia. A little while after, the same governess, who had come to my friend with the highest testimonials of efficiency, and had been twenty years engaged in tuition, having been requested to make her pupil look out in the map the places she read of in history, a practice she had apparently never thought of, was unable to find Numidia on the map of Africa, and on inquiry it turned out that she had looked at the modern map, not knowing the difference between that and the ancient one. When my friend parted with her soon afterwards, expressing her regret that she could not recommend her except as a teacher of music, she said she was aware she ought to apologise for not knowing that Caractacus was a Roman emperor!

The second anecdote illustrates the want of arithmetical knowledge in female teachers. My friend found a lady she was visiting, and her governess non-plussed by the question of her little girl, why in a simple subtraction sum, when she had borrowed ten to enable her to subtract one figure from another, she had to carry one to the next figure.

My friend explained the mystery to the great relief and admiration of the mother and governess.—*M. G. G.*

APPENDIX XVI.

List of Societies and Associations.

1. Scholastic Registration Society (for the Registration of Teachers, Male and Female).

2. Association for Promoting the Application of Endowments to Women.

3. London Association of Schoolmistresses.

4. North of England Council for Promoting the Higher Education of Women, representing Liverpool, Leeds, Manchester, Sheffield, Newcastle, Bradford, Birkenhead, and other towns.

5. Associations of Schoolmistresses in Leeds, Manchester, Sheffield.

6. Manchester Association for Promoting the Education of Women.

7. Birmingham Association for Promoting the Education of Women.

To these may be added as means already in operation,—

The Local Junior and Senior University Examinations for Girls.

The Cambridge Examinations for Women.

Committees in London and in the North of England for Lectures to Ladies.

Classes for Ladies in Clifton, which are almost growing into a College.